BLACK VOICES ON RACE

TONI MORRISON

by Shasta Clinch

FOCUS
READERS.

NAVIGATOR

WWW.FOCUSREADERS.COM

Focus Readers is distributed by North Star Editions:
sales@northstareditions.com | 888-417-0195

Produced for Focus Readers by Red Line Editorial.

Content Consultant: Michon Benson, PhD, Assistant Professor of English, Texas Southern University

Photographs ©: AP Images, cover, 1; Shasta Clinch, 2; Kathy Willens/AP Images, 4–5; Guillermo Arias/AP Images, 7; Bernard Gotfryd/LOC/RBM Vintage Images/Alamy, 8–9; John Collier Jr./Library of Congress, 10; Everett Collection Inc/CSU Archives/Alamy, 12–13; Richard B. Levine/Alamy, 15; Bernard Gotfryd/Library of Congress, 17, 23; David Bookstaver/AP Images, 18–19; Brigitte Friedrich/Süddeutsche Zeitung Photo/Alamy, 20; Rick Bowmer/AP Images, 25; Shutterstock, 26–27; Red Line Editorial, 29

Library of Congress Cataloging-in-Publication Data
Library of Congress Cataloging-in-Publication Data is available on the Library of Congress website.

ISBN
978-1-63739-266-9 (hardcover)
978-1-63739-318-5 (paperback)
978-1-63739-418-2 (ebook pdf)
978-1-63739-370-3 (hosted ebook)

Printed in the United States of America
Mankato, MN
082022

ABOUT THE AUTHOR
Shasta Clinch is a freelance copy editor and proofreader. She lives with her husband and two lovely littles in New Jersey.

TABLE OF CONTENTS

CHAPTER 1

THE POWER OF LANGUAGE

On October 7, 1993, Toni Morrison won the Nobel Prize in Literature. Nobel Prizes honor the amazing achievements of people around the world. The prize in literature honors an author whose whole body of work is outstanding. Morrison won for writing that shows American

Toni Morrison won the Nobel Prize because of the power of her language.

reality. She was the first Black American to win the award.

Morrison gave a speech when she received the prize. She talked about the power of language. People can use language to **oppress**. For example, sexist or racist language is unjust. It prevents people from respecting one another.

People can also use language to uplift. For example, language can inspire people. It can expand people's imaginations. And it can support knowledge. Morrison believed the most important thing about language is how people use it. She considered what people do with language to be a central part of their lives.

Morrison was an influential public speaker and writer.

Morrison used language to teach. She wrote about what it is like to be Black in America. Her books challenge readers to think about the world in new ways. Morrison believed that through words, people can change the world.

CHAPTER 2

GETTING HER START

Toni Morrison was born on February 18, 1931, in Lorain, Ohio. Her parents believed education was important. They taught her to read. She grew up loving stories, especially folklore. Her parents raised her in an **integrated** neighborhood. However, she experienced **segregation** when she went to college.

Toni Morrison was born Chloe Wofford. She changed her first name in college and her last name when she got married.

Howard University is a historically Black university. It was formed in 1867 to provide education to Black Americans.

Morrison attended Howard University in Washington, DC. In that city, people were separated based on their skin color. Morrison saw restaurants in which she could not eat. She saw stores in which she could not shop.

After graduating, Morrison moved to Ithaca, New York. She earned her master's degree in English at Cornell

University. After that, she taught English at two universities. In 1965, Morrison became an editor at Random House, a major **publisher**. Within two years, she became a senior editor. She was the first Black woman to earn that position at Random House.

LIFTING BLACK VOICES

An editor prepares books for publishing. As an editor, Morrison advanced the careers of Black Americans. For example, she edited the work of activist Angela Davis. She worked with author Gayl Jones. And she worked with boxer Muhammad Ali. Morrison aimed to lift Black voices. She wanted their words to speak to Black readers.

CHAPTER 3

WRITING TO REPRESENT

Toni Morrison wrote books while she worked as a professor and editor. Her first novel, *The Bluest Eye*, was published in 1970. It is about a Black girl who wishes she had blue eyes. She never sees people who look like her treated fairly. For this reason, she believes having blue eyes would improve her life. It would also make

Toni Morrison was 39 years old when her first novel was published.

others believe she is pretty. The novel challenges American ideas of beauty. It also shows why representation matters.

REPRESENTATION

Representation is how media show different communities. For example, one movie may **stereotype** Black people. Another movie may show Black people as complex human beings. Representation also has to do with whether communities are featured at all. For instance, a movie with only white actors lacks Black representation. Good representation allows people to see themselves. It confirms that their experiences matter. **Diversity** in media develops people's appreciation for different cultures. It also strengthens people's respect for humankind.

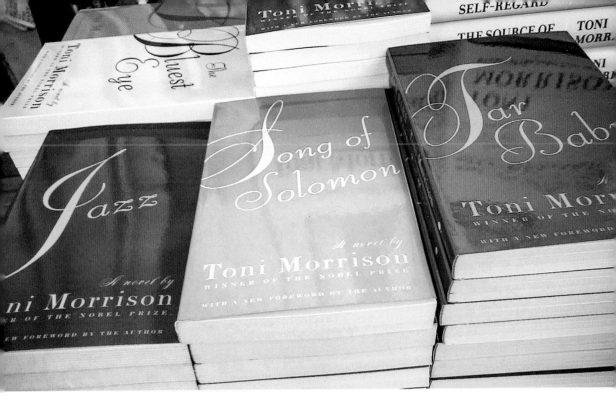

Song of Solomon uses elements of Black American history and folklore to tell a powerful story.

Morrison's next book was published in 1973. *Sula* follows the lives of two Black girls who grow up together. The novel explores friendship, gender, and the thin line between good and evil. Morrison released her next book in 1977. *Song of Solomon* quickly became popular. It was

Morrison's first book with a male main character. In the book, the character learns about his family's history and his own identity. *Song of Solomon* won the National Book Critics Circle Award. It made Morrison famous across the United States.

Because of *Song of Solomon*'s success, Morrison left her job as an editor. She started working full-time as a writer. Morrison had noticed that Black writers often wrote books for white audiences. But she wanted to write books about people who are often overlooked. She wanted to write books *for* these people, too. So, she focused on writing books

From publishing Black authors to writing about Black life, Morrison left a deep impact on American literature.

about Black people for Black audiences. Morrison showed how complex Black American life is. In particular, she explored how Black lives have been shaped by the **legacy** of slavery.

CHAPTER 4

BELOVED

Toni Morrison's fifth novel came out in 1987. *Beloved* is a work of **historical fiction**. It is based on a true story. *Beloved* is about formerly enslaved people. It follows the decisions they make based on their experiences.

Morrison developed the story when she was an editor. While researching for

Toni Morrison poses with a copy of *Beloved* in New York. Many people consider it her best work.

Morrison never avoided difficult topics or themes in her writing.

another book, she read the true story of Margaret Garner. Garner and her family ran away from the man who had enslaved them. This man sent slave catchers to find them. When they were found, Garner refused to be re-enslaved. She also didn't want her children sent back. So, she tried to kill them and herself. One of the children died. Garner was put on trial for the crime.

In *Beloved*, Morrison reimagines Garner as a woman named Sethe. Through Sethe, Morrison shows the horrors of slavery. She also examines what it means to be human in a society that treats some people like property.

Beloved was very popular and highly praised. In 1988, it won the Pulitzer Prize for Fiction. This is one of the top awards in literature. A few years later, Morrison won the Nobel Prize.

Morrison wrote 11 novels in her lifetime. "I didn't want to speak for Black people," she said. "I wanted to speak to, and to be among them." She described the history of Black Americans as "varied,

THE OPRAH WINFREY EFFECT

In 1996, Morrison appeared on *The Oprah Winfrey Show* for the first time. Oprah Winfrey was a famous talk show host. Any books she recommended became extremely popular. Winfrey chose four of Morrison's books for her book club over the years. The books had always sold well. But after Winfrey recommended them, Morrison became even more famous. Ten years after *Beloved* was published, Winfrey made the book into a movie. Winfrey acted in the lead role.

Morrison and her two sons stand near their New York home in the 1980s.

complex and beautiful, and impactful."[1] These feelings come out in her novels. Morrison also wrote several children's books with her son Slade. She wrote many essays, too.

1. *Toni Morrison: The Pieces I Am*. Directed by Timothy Greenfield-Sanders, Magnolia Pictures, 2019.

BANNED BOOKS

Some critics have challenged Toni Morrison's novels. In a challenge, someone tries to limit people's access to a book. For example, someone might ask to take it off the shelves in a library. Or someone might ask to stop teaching about the book in schools. Others have tried to ban Morrison's books. In a ban, the book is actually removed.

Book banning is a form of censorship. Censorship happens when people try to control language. They try to stop something from being said or published.

People challenge books for many reasons. For example, parents might challenge books they think are inappropriate for children. But people often disagree on what is inappropriate.

Morrison's first novel, *The Bluest Eye*, has been frequently challenged. Still, it is widely read, taught, and celebrated.

One example is *The Bluest Eye*. Morrison wrote it in part because of a childhood experience. Her own friend had wanted blue eyes. Parents have challenged the book for its violent scenes. But Morrison was writing about the Black American experience. The truth might be ugly. People might not like it. But that does not make it untrue.

CHAPTER 5

LEGEND AND INSPIRATION

Toni Morrison returned to teaching in 1989. She became a professor at Princeton University. She taught there until 2006. She also continued writing. She wrote up to her death in 2019. During this time, she won many awards.

In 1996, the National Book Foundation honored Morrison. It gave her its Medal

President Barack Obama gives Toni Morrison a medal in 2012.

for Distinguished Contribution to American Letters. The award recognized her lifelong achievements in writing. In 2000, the Library of Congress named Morrison a Living Legend. It honored her again in 2011. It gave her the Creative Achievement Award for Fiction. Then, in 2012, President Barack Obama gave Morrison an award. It was the Presidential Medal of Freedom. This award is the highest honor a US civilian can receive.

Toni Morrison died on August 5, 2019. She was 88 years old. Even after her death, people honored her. For example, in 2020, she was inducted into the National Women's Hall of Fame.

Morrison wrote about Black American life. She made sure to avoid stereotypes. And she showed all sides of what it means to be Black in America. Her work continues to inspire readers and writers all over the world.

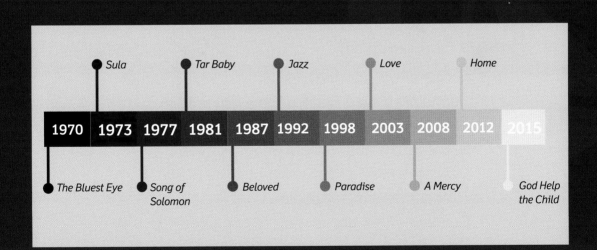

NOVELS BY TONI MORRISON

1970	1973	1977	1981	1987	1992	1998	2003	2008	2012	2015

Above: Sula (1973), Tar Baby (1981), Jazz (1992), Love (2003), Home (2012)

Below: The Bluest Eye (1970), Song of Solomon (1977), Beloved (1987), Paradise (1998), A Mercy (2008), God Help the Child (2015)

FOCUS ON
TONI MORRISON

Write your answers on a separate piece of paper.

1. Write a few sentences summarizing the themes in Toni Morrison's novels.

2. Do you think language is powerful? Why or why not?

3. Which of Morrison's books won the Pulitzer Prize for Fiction?

   A. *Song of Solomon*
   B. *Beloved*
   C. *The Bluest Eye*

4. How did Morrison's novels contribute to Black representation?

   A. She wrote about Black lives and experiences and portrayed Black people as complex human beings.
   B. She wrote about white people's lives and experiences and stereotyped the Black characters in her books.
   C. Some of her books were banned because they made many people uncomfortable.

Answer key on page 32.

GLOSSARY

diversity
The practice of including people from a wide range of backgrounds and identities.

historical fiction
A book that takes place in the past.

integrated
Including people of different races.

legacy
Something that is passed down from what came before.

oppress
To treat someone in a way that is unjust and unfair on purpose.

publisher
A person or company that prepares and prints books and other works for sale.

segregation
The separation of groups of people based on race or other factors.

stereotype
To portray a group of people in a way that oversimplifies and does harm to them.

TO LEARN MORE

BOOKS

Harris, Duchess, and Tammy Gagne. *Richard Wright: Author and World Traveler*. Minneapolis: Abdo Publishing, 2020.

Hegedus, Bethany. *Rise: From Caged Bird to Poet of the People, Maya Angelou*. New York: Lee & Low Books, 2019.

Workneh, Lilly, ed. *Good Night Stories for Rebel Girls: 100 Real-Life Tales of Black Girl Magic*. Los Angeles: Rebel Girls, 2021.

NOTE TO EDUCATORS

Visit **www.focusreaders.com** to find lesson plans, activities, links, and other resources related to this title.

INDEX

Answer Key: 1. Answers will vary; **2.** Answers will vary; **3.** B; **4.** A